◆◆◆◆◆◆◆◆◆◆◆◆◆◆◆◆◆◆◆◆◆◆◆◆◆◆

YOU

ME

BED

NOW

◆◆◆◆◆◆◆◆◆◆◆◆◆◆◆◆◆◆◆◆◆◆◆◆◆◆

CONTINENTS COVERED

FULLY PAINT THE CONTINENT

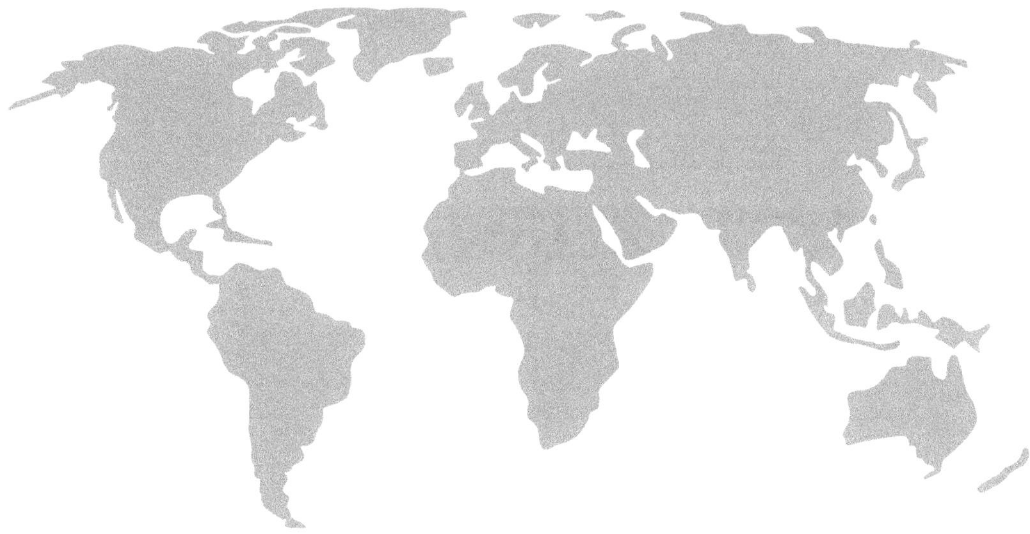

COUNTRIES COVERED

PUT A DOT ON EVERY COUNTRY

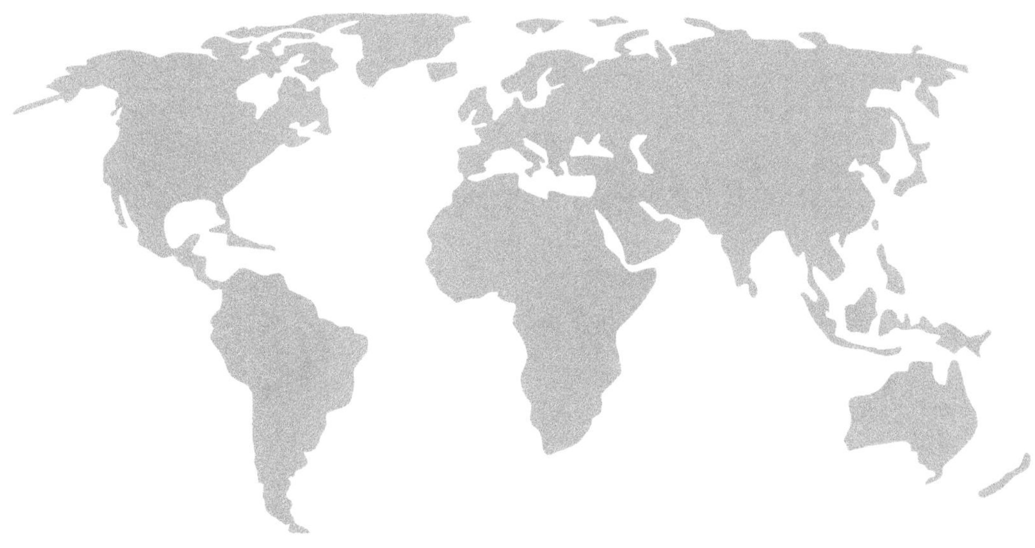

PARTNER 1

Name:_______________________________

Age:____________

Sex:________________

Country:__________________________

WE NEED MORE INFO, HUN

Date: ☐ ☐ ☐　　　　Time: ☐ – ☐

Occasion:_________________________

____

____

____

One Night Stand ☐　　　Friends With Benefits ☐

Partner ☐　　　Complicated ☐

How good was it - Ring in how you felt:

The best thing about this sexual encounter:_____________

____

PARTNER 2

Name:______________________________________

Age:________________

Sex:___________________

Country:_________________________________

Date: ☐ ☐ ☐   Time: ☐ - ☐

Occasion: _________________________________

____

____

____

One Night Stand ☐   Friends With Benefits ☐

Partner ☐   Complicated ☐

How good was it - Ring in how you felt:

The best thing about this sexual encounter: _______________

____

PARTNER 3

Name:_______________________________________

Age:_______________

Sex:_______________________

Country:_______________________________________

WE NEED MORE INFO, HUN

Date: ☐ ☐ ☐   Time: ☐ – ☐

Occasion:_______________________________________

____

____

____

One Night Stand ☐   Friends With Benefits ☐

Partner ☐   Complicated ☐

How good was it - Ring in how you felt:

The best thing about this sexual encounter:_______________

____

PARTNER 4

Name:_______________________________

Age:_____________

Sex:_________________

Country:_____________________________

Date: ☐ ☐ ☐   Time: ☐ – ☐

Occasion: ___________________________

____

____

____

One Night Stand ☐   Friends With Benefits ☐

Partner ☐   Complicated ☐

How good was it - Ring in how you felt:

The best thing about this sexual encounter:_________________

____

PARTNER 5

Name:_______________________________________

Age:________________

Sex:___________________

Country:_________________________________

WE NEED MORE INFO, HUN

Date: ☐ ☐ ☐   Time: ☐ – ☐

Occasion:____

____

____

____

One Night Stand ☐   Friends With Benefits ☐

Partner ☐   Complicated ☐

How good was it - Ring in how you felt:

The best thing about this sexual encounter:_______________

____

PARTNER 6

Name:_______________________________________

Age:_______________

Sex:_____________________

Country:_________________________________

WE NEED MORE INFO, HUN

Date: ☐ ☐ ☐   Time: ☐ - ☐

Occasion: _________________________________

____

____

____

One Night Stand ☐   Friends With Benefits ☐

Partner ☐   Complicated ☐

How good was it - Ring in how you felt:

The best thing about this sexual encounter: _______________

____

PARTNER 7

Name:_______________________________________

Age:_______________

Sex:_____________________

Country:___________________________________

WE NEED MORE INFO, HUN

Date: ☐ ☐ ☐   Time: ☐ – ☐

Occasion:_________________________________

____

____

____

One Night Stand ☐   Friends With Benefits ☐

Partner ☐   Complicated ☐

How good was it - Ring in how you felt:

The best thing about this sexual encounter:_______________

____

PARTNER 8

Name:______________________________________

Age:______________

Sex:__________________

Country:____________________________________

Date: ☐ ☐ ☐   Time: ☐ – ☐

Occasion: __________________________________

____

____

____

| One Night Stand ☐ | Friends With Benefits ☐ |
| Partner ☐ | Complicated ☐ |

How good was it - Ring in how you felt:

The best thing about this sexual encounter:______________

____

PARTNER 9

Name:_______________________________________

Age:_______________

Sex:_______________

Country:_______________________________

WE NEED MORE INFO, HUN

Date: ☐ ☐ ☐   Time: ☐ – ☐

Occasion:_______________________________

____

____

____

One Night Stand ☐   Friends With Benefits ☐

Partner ☐   Complicated ☐

How good was it - Ring in how you felt:

The best thing about this sexual encounter:_______________

____

PARTNER 10

Name:_______________________________________

Age:______________________

Sex:_____________________________

Country:____

Date: ☐ ☐ ☐   Time: ☐ – ☐

Occasion: ____

____

____

____

One Night Stand ☐   Friends With Benefits ☐

Partner ☐   Complicated ☐

How good was it - Ring in how you felt:

The best thing about this sexual encounter: ________________

____

PARTNER 11

Name:_______________________________________

Age:_______________

Sex:___________________________

Country:_________________________________

WE NEED MORE INFO, HUN

Date: ☐ ☐ ☐   Time: ☐ – ☐

Occasion:_________________________________

____

____

____

One Night Stand ☐   Friends With Benefits ☐

Partner ☐   Complicated ☐

How good was it - Ring in how you felt:

The best thing about this sexual encounter:_______________

____

PARTNER 12

Name:_______________________________________

Age:_______________

Sex:___________________

Country:_______________________________________

Date: ▢ ▢ ▢   Time: ▢ – ▢

Occasion: ___________________________________

____

____

____

One Night Stand ▢   Friends With Benefits ▢

Partner ▢   Complicated ▢

How good was it - Ring in how you felt:

The best thing about this sexual encounter:_______________

____

PARTNER 13

Name:_______________________________________

Age:_______________

Sex:_____________________________

Country:___________________________________

WE NEED MORE INFO, HUN

Date: ☐ ☐ ☐   Time: ☐ – ☐

Occasion:__________________________________

____

____

____

One Night Stand ☐   Friends With Benefits ☐

Partner ☐   Complicated ☐

How good was it - Ring in how you felt:

The best thing about this sexual encounter:_________________

____

PARTNER 14

Name:_______________________________

Age:_______________

Sex:___________________________

Country:_________________________________

Date: ☐ ☐ ☐   Time: ☐ – ☐

Occasion: _________________________________

____

____

____

One Night Stand ☐   Friends With Benefits ☐

Partner ☐   Complicated ☐

How good was it - Ring in how you felt:

The best thing about this sexual encounter:_________________

____

PARTNER 15

Name:_______________________________________

Age:_______________

Sex:___________________

Country:_________________________________

Date: ☐ ☐ ☐   Time: ☐ – ☐

Occasion:________________________________

____

____

____

One Night Stand ☐   Friends With Benefits ☐

Partner ☐   Complicated ☐

How good was it - Ring in how you felt:

The best thing about this sexual encounter:_______________

____

PARTNER 16

Name:_____________________________________

Age:______________

Sex:___________________

Country:_______________________________

Date: ☐ ☐ ☐   Time: ☐ - ☐

Occasion: _________________________________

____

____

____

One Night Stand ☐   Friends With Benefits ☐

Partner ☐   Complicated ☐

How good was it - Ring in how you felt:

The best thing about this sexual encounter: _______________

____

PARTNER 17

Name:_______________________________________

Age:_______________

Sex:_________________

Country:____________________________

WE NEED MORE INFO, HUN

Date: ☐ ☐ ☐   Time: ☐ – ☐

Occasion:_____________________________

____

____

____

| One Night Stand ☐ | Friends With Benefits ☐ |
| Partner ☐ | Complicated ☐ |

How good was it - Ring in how you felt:

😟 😬 😅 😄 😝 😍

The best thing about this sexual encounter: _______________

____

PARTNER 18

Name:_______________________________________

Age:_______________

Sex:_____________________________

Country:_______________________________________

WE NEED MORE INFO, HUN

Date: ☐ ☐ ☐   Time: ☐ – ☐

Occasion: _______________________________________

____

____

____

One Night Stand ☐   Friends With Benefits ☐

Partner ☐   Complicated ☐

How good was it - Ring in how you felt:

The best thing about this sexual encounter:_______________________________________

____

PARTNER 19

Name:____

Age:________________

Sex:____________________

Country:________________________________

WE NEED MORE INFO, HUN

Date: ☐ ☐ ☐　　　　　　Time: ☐ – ☐

Occasion:________________________________

____

____

____

One Night Stand ☐　　　　Friends With Benefits ☐

Partner ☐　　　　Complicated ☐

How good was it - Ring in how you felt:

The best thing about this sexual encounter:________________________

____

PARTNER 20

Name:____

Age:_______________

Sex:___________________

Country:___________________________________

Date: ☐ ☐ ☐   Time: ☐ – ☐

Occasion: ______________________________________

____

____

____

One Night Stand ☐   Friends With Benefits ☐

Partner ☐   Complicated ☐

How good was it - Ring in how you felt:

The best thing about this sexual encounter:_______________

____

PARTNER 21

Name:_______________________________________

Age:_______________

Sex:_____________________

Country:_______________________________

WE NEED MORE INFO, HUN

Date: ☐ ☐ ☐   Time: ☐ – ☐

Occasion:_______________________________

____

____

____

One Night Stand ☐   Friends With Benefits ☐

Partner ☐   Complicated ☐

How good was it - Ring in how you felt:

The best thing about this sexual encounter:_______________

____

PARTNER 22

Name:_______________________________________

Age:________________

Sex:___________________

Country:_________________________________

Date: ☐ ☐ ☐   Time: ☐ – ☐

Occasion: _________________________________

____

____

____

One Night Stand ☐   Friends With Benefits ☐

Partner ☐   Complicated ☐

How good was it - Ring in how you felt:

The best thing about this sexual encounter:_______________

____

PARTNER 23

Name:____

Age:_______________

Sex:___________________________

Country:____

WE NEED MORE INFO, HUN

Date: ☐ ☐ ☐   Time: ☐ – ☐

Occasion:____

____

____

____

One Night Stand ☐   Friends With Benefits ☐

Partner ☐   Complicated ☐

How good was it - Ring in how you felt:

😟 😬 😅 😄 😋 😍

The best thing about this sexual encounter:_______________

____

PARTNER 24

Name:_______________________________________

Age:_______________

Sex:_____________________

Country:___________________________________

WE NEED MORE INFO, HUN

Date: ☐ ☐ ☐   Time: ☐ – ☐

Occasion: _________________________________

____

____

____

One Night Stand ☐   Friends With Benefits ☐

Partner ☐   Complicated ☐

How good was it - Ring in how you felt:

The best thing about this sexual encounter:_______________

____

PARTNER 25

Name:____

Age:_______________

Sex:___________________________

Country:_______________________________________

Date: ☐ ☐ ☐   Time: ☐ - ☐

Occasion:____

____

____

____

One Night Stand ☐   Friends With Benefits ☐

Partner ☐   Complicated ☐

How good was it - Ring in how you felt:

The best thing about this sexual encounter:_______________

____

PARTNER 26

Name:_______________________________________

Age:________________

Sex:___________________________

Country:____

WE NEED MORE INFO, HUN

Date: ☐ ☐ ☐   Time: ☐ - ☐

Occasion: ____

____

____

____

One Night Stand ☐   Friends With Benefits ☐

Partner ☐   Complicated ☐

How good was it - Ring in how you felt:

The best thing about this sexual encounter:_________________

____

PARTNER 27

Name:_______________________________________

Age:_______________

Sex:_________________

Country:_________________________________

Date: ☐ ☐ ☐   Time: ☐ – ☐

Occasion:_____________________________________

____

____

____

One Night Stand ☐   Friends With Benefits ☐

Partner ☐   Complicated ☐

How good was it - Ring in how you felt:

The best thing about this sexual encounter:_______________

____

PARTNER 28

Name:_______________________________________

Age:_______________

Sex:_____________________

Country:___________________________________

WE NEED MORE INFO, HUN

Date: ☐ ☐ ☐   Time: ☐ – ☐

Occasion: _________________________________

____

____

____

One Night Stand ☐   Friends With Benefits ☐

Partner ☐   Complicated ☐

How good was it - Ring in how you felt:

The best thing about this sexual encounter:______________

____

PARTNER 29

Name:____

Age:_______________

Sex:__________________

Country:_____________________________

Date: ☐ ☐ ☐   Time: ☐ – ☐

Occasion:_____________________________

____

____

____

One Night Stand ☐   Friends With Benefits ☐

Partner ☐   Complicated ☐

How good was it - Ring in how you felt:

The best thing about this sexual encounter:_______________

____

PARTNER 30

Name:_______________________________

Age:_______________

Sex:___________________________

Country:_______________________________

Date: ☐ ☐ ☐   Time: ☐ – ☐

Occasion: _________________________________

____

____

____

One Night Stand ☐   Friends With Benefits ☐

Partner ☐   Complicated ☐

How good was it - Ring in how you felt:

The best thing about this sexual encounter:_______________

____

PARTNER 31

Name:____

Age:_______________

Sex:_________________________

Country:____

WE NEED MORE INFO, HUN

Date: ☐ ☐ ☐   Time: ☐ – ☐

Occasion:____

____

____

____

One Night Stand ☐   Friends With Benefits ☐

Partner ☐   Complicated ☐

How good was it - Ring in how you felt:

The best thing about this sexual encounter:_________________

____

PARTNER 32

Name:_______________________________

Age:___________

Sex:________________

Country:_______________________________

WE NEED MORE INFO, HUN

Date: ☐ ☐ ☐   Time: ☐ - ☐

Occasion: _______________________________

____

____

____

One Night Stand ☐   Friends With Benefits ☐

Partner ☐   Complicated ☐

How good was it - Ring in how you felt:

The best thing about this sexual encounter:_______________________________

____

PARTNER 33

Name:_______________________________________

Age:_______________

Sex:_____________________________

Country:_________________________________

WE NEED MORE INFO, HUN

Date: ☐ ☐ ☐   Time: ☐ – ☐

Occasion:_________________________________

____

____

____

One Night Stand ☐   Friends With Benefits ☐

Partner ☐   Complicated ☐

How good was it - Ring in how you felt:

The best thing about this sexual encounter:_______________

____

PARTNER 34

Name:_________________________________

Age:_____________

Sex:_________________

Country:_______________________

Date: ☐ ☐ ☐   Time: ☐ - ☐

Occasion: _______________________

____

____

____

One Night Stand ☐   Friends With Benefits ☐

Partner ☐   Complicated ☐

How good was it - Ring in how you felt:

The best thing about this sexual encounter:_______________________

____

PARTNER 35

Name:_______________________________________

Age:_______________

Sex:_________________________

Country:_________________________________

Date: ☐ ☐ ☐   Time: ☐ – ☐

Occasion:_________________________________

____

____

____

| One Night Stand ☐ | Friends With Benefits ☐ |
| Partner ☐ | Complicated ☐ |

How good was it - Ring in how you felt:

The best thing about this sexual encounter:_________________

____

PARTNER 36

Name:_______________________________________

Age:_______________

Sex:___________________________

Country:____

Date: ☐ ☐ ☐   Time: ☐ – ☐

Occasion: ____

____

____

____

One Night Stand ☐   Friends With Benefits ☐

Partner ☐   Complicated ☐

How good was it - Ring in how you felt:

The best thing about this sexual encounter:_______________

____

PARTNER 37

Name:_______________________________________

Age:_______________

Sex:__________________________

Country:_______________________________________

WE NEED MORE INFO, HUN

Date: ☐ ☐ ☐   Time: ☐ – ☐

Occasion:_______________________________________

____

____

____

One Night Stand ☐   Friends With Benefits ☐

Partner ☐   Complicated ☐

How good was it - Ring in how you felt:

The best thing about this sexual encounter:_______________

____

PARTNER 38

Name:_______________________________________

Age:_______________

Sex:___________________________

Country:____

WE NEED MORE INFO, HUN

Date: ☐ ☐ ☐   Time: ☐ - ☐

Occasion: ____

____

____

____

One Night Stand ☐   Friends With Benefits ☐

Partner ☐   Complicated ☐

How good was it - Ring in how you felt:

The best thing about this sexual encounter:_______________

____

PARTNER 39

Name:____

Age:________________

Sex:__________________

Country:________________________________

Date: ☐ ☐ ☐   Time: ☐ – ☐

Occasion:_______________________________________

____

____

____

One Night Stand ☐   Friends With Benefits ☐

Partner ☐   Complicated ☐

How good was it - Ring in how you felt:

The best thing about this sexual encounter:_______________

____

PARTNER 40

Name:_______________________________________

Age:_______________

Sex:___________________

Country:_________________________________

WE NEED MORE INFO, HUN

Date: ☐ ☐ ☐   Time: ☐ – ☐

Occasion: _________________________________

____

____

____

One Night Stand ☐   Friends With Benefits ☐

Partner ☐   Complicated ☐

How good was it - Ring in how you felt:

The best thing about this sexual encounter:_________________

____

PARTNER 41

Name:____

Age:_______________

Sex:___________________

Country:_________________________________

WE NEED MORE INFO, HUN

Date: ☐ ☐ ☐   Time: ☐ – ☐

Occasion:_________________________________

____

____

____

One Night Stand ☐   Friends With Benefits ☐

Partner ☐   Complicated ☐

How good was it - Ring in how you felt:

The best thing about this sexual encounter:_________________

____

PARTNER 42

Name:_______________________________

Age:_______________

Sex:__________________

Country:_______________________________

WE NEED MORE INFO, HUN

Date: ☐ ☐ ☐   Time: ☐ – ☐

Occasion: _______________________________

____

____

____

One Night Stand ☐   Friends With Benefits ☐

Partner ☐   Complicated ☐

How good was it - Ring in how you felt:

The best thing about this sexual encounter:_______________________________

____

PARTNER 43

Name:_______________________________________

Age:_______________

Sex:___________________

Country:_________________________________

WE NEED MORE INFO, HUN

Date: ☐ ☐ ☐   Time: ☐ – ☐

Occasion:_______________________________________

____

____

____

One Night Stand ☐   Friends With Benefits ☐

Partner ☐   Complicated ☐

How good was it - Ring in how you felt:

The best thing about this sexual encounter:_______________________

____

PARTNER 44

Name:_______________________________________

Age:_______________

Sex:___________________________

Country:____

Date: ☐ ☐ ☐   Time: ☐ – ☐

Occasion: ____________________________________

____

____

____

One Night Stand ☐   Friends With Benefits ☐

Partner ☐   Complicated ☐

How good was it - Ring in how you felt:

The best thing about this sexual encounter:________________

____

PARTNER 45

Name:_______________________________________

Age:_______________

Sex:__________________

Country:_______________________________

WE NEED MORE INFO, HUN

Date: ☐ ☐ ☐ Time: ☐ – ☐

Occasion:_______________________________

____

____

____

One Night Stand ☐   Friends With Benefits ☐

Partner ☐   Complicated ☐

How good was it - Ring in how you felt:

The best thing about this sexual encounter:_______________

____

PARTNER 46

Name:_______________________________

Age:____________

Sex:____________________

Country:_______________________________

Date: ☐ ☐ ☐   Time: ☐ - ☐

Occasion: _______________________________

____

____

____

One Night Stand ☐   Friends With Benefits ☐

Partner ☐   Complicated ☐

How good was it - Ring in how you felt:

The best thing about this sexual encounter:_______________

____

PARTNER 47

Name:_______________________________________

Age:______________

Sex:_________________________

Country:_________________________________

WE NEED MORE INFO, HUN

Date: ☐ ☐ ☐   Time: ☐ – ☐

Occasion:_________________________________

____

____

____

One Night Stand ☐   Friends With Benefits ☐

Partner ☐   Complicated ☐

How good was it - Ring in how you felt:

The best thing about this sexual encounter:_________________

____

PARTNER 48

Name:____

Age:_________________

Sex:___________________

Country:____

WE NEED MORE INFO, HUN

Date: ☐ ☐ ☐   Time: ☐ – ☐

Occasion: ______________________________________

____

____

____

One Night Stand ☐	Friends With Benefits ☐
Partner ☐	Complicated ☐

How good was it - Ring in how you felt:

The best thing about this sexual encounter:______________

____

PARTNER 49

Name:____

Age:______________

Sex:__________________________

Country:_________________________________

WE NEED MORE INFO, HUN

Date: ☐ ☐ ☐   Time: ☐ – ☐

Occasion:_________________________________

____

____

____

One Night Stand ☐   Friends With Benefits ☐

Partner ☐   Complicated ☐

How good was it - Ring in how you felt:

The best thing about this sexual encounter:_________________

____

PARTNER 50

Name:________________________________

Age:______________

Sex:__________________

Country:______________________________

WE NEED MORE INFO, HUN

Date: ☐ ☐ ☐   Time: ☐ - ☐

Occasion: ___________________________

____

____

____

One Night Stand ☐   Friends With Benefits ☐

Partner ☐   Complicated ☐

How good was it - Ring in how you felt:

The best thing about this sexual encounter:____________

____

PARTNER 51

Name:_______________________________________

Age:________________

Sex:___________________

Country:_________________________________

WE NEED MORE INFO, HUN

Date: ☐ ☐ ☐   Time: ☐ – ☐

Occasion:________________________________

____

____

____

One Night Stand ☐   Friends With Benefits ☐

Partner ☐   Complicated ☐

How good was it - Ring in how you felt:

The best thing about this sexual encounter:_______________

____

PARTNER 52

Name:_______________________________________

Age:_______________

Sex:___________________

Country:_________________________________

Date: ☐ ☐ ☐   Time: ☐ – ☐

Occasion: _______________________________

____

____

____

One Night Stand ☐   Friends With Benefits ☐

Partner ☐   Complicated ☐

How good was it - Ring in how you felt:

The best thing about this sexual encounter:_______________

____

PARTNER 53

Name:_______________________________________

Age:_______________

Sex:_________________________

Country:_________________________________

WE NEED MORE INFO, HUN

Date: ☐ ☐ ☐   Time: ☐ – ☐

Occasion:_________________________________

____

____

____

One Night Stand ☐   Friends With Benefits ☐

Partner ☐   Complicated ☐

How good was it - Ring in how you felt:

The best thing about this sexual encounter:_________________

____

PARTNER 54

Name:

Age:

Sex:

Country:

Date: Time:

Occasion:

One Night Stand   Friends With Benefits

Partner   Complicated

How good was it - Ring in how you felt:

The best thing about this sexual encounter:

PARTNER 55

Name:_______________________________________

Age:_______________

Sex:___________________

Country:_________________________________

WE NEED MORE INFO, HUN

Date: ☐ ☐ ☐   Time: ☐ – ☐

Occasion:_________________________________

____

____

____

One Night Stand ☐   Friends With Benefits ☐

Partner ☐   Complicated ☐

How good was it - Ring in how you felt:

The best thing about this sexual encounter: _______________

____

PARTNER 56

Name:_______________________________

Age:_______________

Sex:___________________

Country:_______________________________

Date: ☐ ☐ ☐   Time: ☐ – ☐

Occasion: _______________________________

____

____

____

One Night Stand ☐   Friends With Benefits ☐

Partner ☐   Complicated ☐

How good was it - Ring in how you felt:

The best thing about this sexual encounter:_______________

____

PARTNER 57

Name:____

Age:_______________

Sex:___________________

Country:___________________________________

Date: ☐ ☐ ☐☐☐☐   Time: ☐ – ☐

Occasion:____

____

____

____

One Night Stand ☐   Friends With Benefits ☐

Partner ☐   Complicated ☐

How good was it - Ring in how you felt:

The best thing about this sexual encounter: _______________

____

PARTNER 58

Name:________________________________

Age:________________

Sex:____________________

Country:________________________________

WE NEED MORE INFO, HUN

Date: ☐ ☐ ☐   Time: ☐ – ☐

Occasion: ________________________________

____

____

____

One Night Stand ☐   Friends With Benefits ☐

Partner ☐   Complicated ☐

How good was it - Ring in how you felt:

The best thing about this sexual encounter:________________

____

PARTNER 59

Name:_______________________________

Age:_______________

Sex:__________________

Country:_____________________________

WE NEED MORE INFO, HUN

Date: ☐ ☐ ☐ Time: ☐ – ☐

Occasion:____________________________

____

____

____

One Night Stand ☐ Friends With Benefits ☐

Partner ☐ Complicated ☐

How good was it - Ring in how you felt:

The best thing about this sexual encounter:_______________

____

PARTNER 60

Name:_______________________________

Age:_______________

Sex:_________________________

Country:_______________________________

Date: ☐ ☐ ☐   Time: ☐ – ☐

Occasion: _______________________________

____

____

____

One Night Stand ☐   Friends With Benefits ☐

Partner ☐   Complicated ☐

How good was it - Ring in how you felt:

The best thing about this sexual encounter:_______________________________

____

PARTNER 61

Name:_______________________________________

Age:________________

Sex:__________________________

Country:_________________________________

Date: ☐ ☐ ☐　　　　Time: ☐ – ☐

Occasion:_________________________________

____

____

____

One Night Stand ☐　　　Friends With Benefits ☐

Partner ☐　　　Complicated ☐

How good was it - Ring in how you felt:

The best thing about this sexual encounter:_______________

____

PARTNER 62

Name:

Age:

Sex:

Country:

WE NEED MORE INFO, HUN

Date: ☐ ☐ ☐   Time: ☐ - ☐

Occasion:

One Night Stand ☐   Friends With Benefits ☐

Partner ☐   Complicated ☐

How good was it - Ring in how you felt:

The best thing about this sexual encounter:

PARTNER 63

Name:______________________________________

Age:_______________

Sex:___________________

Country:________________________________

WE NEED MORE INFO, HUN

Date: ☐ ☐ ☐   Time: ☐ – ☐

Occasion:_________________________________

____

____

____

One Night Stand ☐   Friends With Benefits ☐

Partner ☐   Complicated ☐

How good was it - Ring in how you felt:

The best thing about this sexual encounter:_______________

____

PARTNER 64

Name:_____________________________________

Age:_______________

Sex:___________________

Country:_________________________________

Date: ☐ ☐ ☐   Time: ☐ – ☐

Occasion: _________________________________

____

____

____

One Night Stand ☐   Friends With Benefits ☐

Partner ☐   Complicated ☐

How good was it - Ring in how you felt:

The best thing about this sexual encounter:_____________

____

PARTNER 65

Name:____

Age:______________

Sex:__________________________

Country:____

WE NEED MORE INFO, HUN

Date: ☐ ☐ ☐   Time: ☐ – ☐

Occasion:____

____

____

____

One Night Stand ☐   Friends With Benefits ☐

Partner ☐   Complicated ☐

How good was it - Ring in how you felt:

The best thing about this sexual encounter: __________________

____

PARTNER 66

Name:_______________________________

Age:_______________

Sex:___________________

Country:_______________________________

Date: ☐ ☐ ☐   Time: ☐ – ☐

Occasion: _______________________________

____

____

____

One Night Stand ☐   Friends With Benefits ☐

Partner ☐   Complicated ☐

How good was it - Ring in how you felt:

The best thing about this sexual encounter:_______________________________

____

PARTNER 67

Name:_______________________________________

Age:______________

Sex:_________________

Country:_______________________________

Date: ☐ ☐ ☐   Time: ☐ – ☐

Occasion:_______________________________

____

____

____

One Night Stand ☐   Friends With Benefits ☐

Partner ☐   Complicated ☐

How good was it - Ring in how you felt:

The best thing about this sexual encounter:_______________

____

PARTNER 68

Name:_______________________________

Age:_______________

Sex:_________________________

Country:_______________________________

WE NEED MORE INFO, HUN

Date: ☐ ☐ ☐   Time: ☐ – ☐

Occasion: _______________________________

____

____

____

One Night Stand ☐   Friends With Benefits ☐

Partner ☐   Complicated ☐

How good was it - Ring in how you felt:

The best thing about this sexual encounter: _______________

____

PARTNER 69

Name:____

Age:________________

Sex:____________________________

Country:____

WE NEED MORE INFO, HUN

Date: ☐ ☐ ☐   Time: ☐ – ☐

Occasion:____

____

____

____

One Night Stand ☐   Friends With Benefits ☐

Partner ☐   Complicated ☐

How good was it - Ring in how you felt:

The best thing about this sexual encounter:_______________

____

PARTNER 70

Name:_______________________________________

Age:_______________

Sex:___________________________

Country:____

WE NEED MORE INFO, HUN

Date: ☐ ☐ ☐   Time: ☐ – ☐

Occasion: ____

____

____

____

One Night Stand ☐   Friends With Benefits ☐

Partner ☐   Complicated ☐

How good was it - Ring in how you felt:

The best thing about this sexual encounter:_________________________

____

PARTNER 71

Name:____________________________________

Age:______________

Sex:__________________

Country:________________________________

WE NEED MORE INFO, HUN

Date: ☐ ☐ ☐   Time: ☐ – ☐

Occasion:________________________________

____

____

____

One Night Stand ☐   Friends With Benefits ☐

Partner ☐   Complicated ☐

How good was it - Ring in how you felt:

The best thing about this sexual encounter:____________

____

PARTNER 72

Name:_______________________________________

Age:_______________

Sex:___________________________

Country:____

WE NEED MORE INFO, HUN

Date: ☐ ☐ ☐　　　　Time: ☐ – ☐

Occasion: ______________________________________

____

____

____

One Night Stand ☐　　　　Friends With Benefits ☐

Partner ☐　　　　Complicated ☐

How good was it - Ring in how you felt:

The best thing about this sexual encounter:_________________

____

PARTNER 73

Name:_______________________________________

Age:_______________

Sex:___________________________

Country:____

WE NEED MORE INFO, HUN

Date: ☐ ☐ ☐   Time: ☐ – ☐

Occasion:____

____

____

____

One Night Stand ☐   Friends With Benefits ☐

Partner ☐   Complicated ☐

How good was it - Ring in how you felt:

The best thing about this sexual encounter:___________

____

PARTNER 74

Name:_______________________________

Age:_______________

Sex:_______________

Country:_______________________________

Date: ☐ ☐ ☐   Time: ☐ - ☐

Occasion: _______________________________

____

____

____

One Night Stand ☐   Friends With Benefits ☐

Partner ☐   Complicated ☐

How good was it - Ring in how you felt:

The best thing about this sexual encounter:_______________

____

PARTNER 75

Name:_______________________________

Age:_______________

Sex:_______________

Country:___________________________

Date: ☐ ☐ ☐   Time: ☐ – ☐

Occasion:_________________________________

____

____

____

One Night Stand ☐   Friends With Benefits ☐

Partner ☐   Complicated ☐

How good was it - Ring in how you felt:

The best thing about this sexual encounter:_______________

____

PARTNER 76

Name:_______________________________________

Age:_______________

Sex:__________________

Country:_______________________________________

Date: ☐ ☐ ☐   Time: ☐ – ☐

Occasion: _______________________________________

____

____

____

One Night Stand ☐   Friends With Benefits ☐

Partner ☐   Complicated ☐

How good was it - Ring in how you felt:

The best thing about this sexual encounter:_______________

____

PARTNER 77

Name:____

Age:________________

Sex:__________________

Country:______________________________

WE NEED MORE INFO, HUN

Date: ☐ ☐ ☐   Time: ☐ – ☐

Occasion:______________________________

____

____

____

One Night Stand ☐   Friends With Benefits ☐

Partner ☐   Complicated ☐

How good was it - Ring in how you felt:

The best thing about this sexual encounter: ______________

____

PARTNER 78

Name:____

Age:______________

Sex:__________________________

Country:____

WE NEED MORE INFO, HUN

Date: ☐ ☐ ☐   Time: ☐ – ☐

Occasion: ____

____

____

____

One Night Stand ☐   Friends With Benefits ☐

Partner ☐   Complicated ☐

How good was it - Ring in how you felt:

The best thing about this sexual encounter:________________

____

PARTNER 79

Name:____

Age:________________

Sex:____________________

Country:____

WE NEED MORE INFO, HUN

Date: ☐ ☐ ☐   Time: ☐ – ☐

Occasion:____

____

____

____

One Night Stand ☐   Friends With Benefits ☐

Partner ☐   Complicated ☐

How good was it - Ring in how you felt:

The best thing about this sexual encounter:________________________

____

PARTNER 80

Name:____

Age:________________

Sex:__________________________

Country:____

Date: ☐ ☐ ☐   Time: ☐ – ☐

Occasion: ____

____

____

____

One Night Stand ☐   Friends With Benefits ☐

Partner ☐   Complicated ☐

How good was it - Ring in how you felt:

The best thing about this sexual encounter:________________

____

PARTNER 81

Name:_______________________________

Age:_______________

Sex:_________________________

Country:_____________________________

WE NEED MORE INFO, HUN

Date: ☐ ☐ ☐   Time: ☐ – ☐

Occasion:____________________________

____

____

____

One Night Stand ☐   Friends With Benefits ☐

Partner ☐   Complicated ☐

How good was it - Ring in how you felt:

The best thing about this sexual encounter:____________

____

PARTNER 82

Name:_______________________________________

Age:________________

Sex:____________________

Country:___________________________________

Date: □ □ □   Time: □ - □

Occasion: _________________________________

____

____

____

One Night Stand □   Friends With Benefits □

Partner □   Complicated □

How good was it - Ring in how you felt:

The best thing about this sexual encounter:_______________

____

PARTNER 83

Name:_______________________________

Age:_______________

Sex:_________________

Country:_______________________________

WE NEED MORE INFO, HUN

Date: ☐ ☐ ☐   Time: ☐ – ☐

Occasion:_______________________________

____

____

____

One Night Stand ☐   Friends With Benefits ☐

Partner ☐   Complicated ☐

How good was it - Ring in how you felt:

The best thing about this sexual encounter:_______________________________

____

PARTNER 84

Name:____

Age:________________________

Sex:_______________________________

Country:____

Date: ☐ ☐ ☐   Time: ☐ – ☐

Occasion: ____

____

____

____

One Night Stand ☐   Friends With Benefits ☐

Partner ☐   Complicated ☐

How good was it - Ring in how you felt:

The best thing about this sexual encounter:_______________

____

PARTNER 85

Name:_______________________________________

Age:_______________

Sex:_________________________

Country:__________________________________

Date: ☐ ☐ ☐   Time: ☐ – ☐

Occasion:_________________________________

____

____

____

One Night Stand ☐   Friends With Benefits ☐

Partner ☐   Complicated ☐

How good was it - Ring in how you felt:

The best thing about this sexual encounter: _______________

____

PARTNER 86

Name:_______________________________

Age:_____________

Sex:________________________

Country:_________________________________

WE NEED MORE INFO, HUN

Date: ☐ ☐ ☐   Time: ☐ - ☐

Occasion: _________________________________

____

____

____

| One Night Stand ☐ | Friends With Benefits ☐ |
| Partner ☐ | Complicated ☐ |

How good was it - Ring in how you felt:

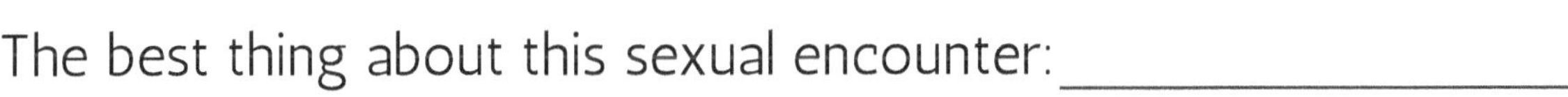

The best thing about this sexual encounter:_____________

____

PARTNER 87

Name:_____________________________

Age:__________

Sex:______________

Country:________________________

WE NEED MORE INFO, HUN

Date: ☐ ☐ ☐   Time: ☐ – ☐

Occasion:_______________________

____

____

____

One Night Stand ☐   Friends With Benefits ☐

Partner ☐   Complicated ☐

How good was it - Ring in how you felt:

The best thing about this sexual encounter:_______________

____

PARTNER 88

Name:________________________________

Age:______________

Sex:__________________

Country:________________________________

Date: ☐ ☐ ☐   Time: ☐ - ☐

Occasion: ________________________________

____

____

____

One Night Stand ☐   Friends With Benefits ☐

Partner ☐   Complicated ☐

How good was it - Ring in how you felt:

The best thing about this sexual encounter:________________

____

PARTNER 89

Name:____

Age:_______________

Sex:___________________________

Country:_________________________________

WE NEED MORE INFO, HUN

Date: ☐ ☐ ☐   Time: ☐ – ☐

Occasion:_________________________________

____

____

____

| One Night Stand ☐ | Friends With Benefits ☐ |
| Partner ☐ | Complicated ☐ |

How good was it - Ring in how you felt:

The best thing about this sexual encounter:_______________

____

PARTNER 90

Name:_______________________________

Age:_______________

Sex:_______________________

Country:_________________________________

Date: ☐ ☐ ☐   Time: ☐ – ☐

Occasion: _________________________________

____

____

____

One Night Stand ☐   Friends With Benefits ☐

Partner ☐   Complicated ☐

How good was it - Ring in how you felt:

The best thing about this sexual encounter:_________________

____

PARTNER 91

Name:_______________________________________

Age:_______________

Sex:_______________

Country:_______________________________

WE NEED MORE INFO, HUN

Date: □ □ □   Time: □ – □

Occasion:_______________________________

____

____

____

One Night Stand □   Friends With Benefits □

Partner □   Complicated □

How good was it - Ring in how you felt:

The best thing about this sexual encounter: _______________

____

PARTNER 92

Name:_______________________________________

Age:_______________

Sex:___________________

Country:___________________________________

Date: ☐ ☐ ☐   Time: ☐ – ☐

Occasion: _________________________________

____

____

____

One Night Stand ☐   Friends With Benefits ☐

Partner ☐   Complicated ☐

How good was it - Ring in how you felt:

The best thing about this sexual encounter:_______________

____

PARTNER 93

Name:_______________________________________

Age:_______________

Sex:___________________

Country:_______________________________

WE NEED MORE INFO, HUN

Date: ☐ ☐ ☐   Time: ☐ – ☐

Occasion:_____________________________________

____

____

____

One Night Stand ☐   Friends With Benefits ☐

Partner ☐   Complicated ☐

How good was it - Ring in how you felt:

The best thing about this sexual encounter: _______________

____

PARTNER 94

Name:_______________________________

Age:___________

Sex:_______________

Country:_______________________

Date: ☐ ☐ ☐   Time: ☐ – ☐

Occasion: _______________________

____

____

____

One Night Stand ☐   Friends With Benefits ☐

Partner ☐   Complicated ☐

How good was it - Ring in how you felt:

The best thing about this sexual encounter:_______________________

____

PARTNER 95

Name:____

Age:________________

Sex:__________________________

Country:__________________________________

WE NEED MORE INFO, HUN

Date: ☐ ☐ ☐   Time: ☐ – ☐

Occasion:_________________________________

____

____

____

One Night Stand ☐   Friends With Benefits ☐

Partner ☐   Complicated ☐

How good was it - Ring in how you felt:

The best thing about this sexual encounter:_______________

____

PARTNER 96

Name:_______________________________________

Age:_______________

Sex:_________________

Country:___________________________________

WE NEED MORE INFO, HUN

Date: ☐ ☐ ☐   Time: ☐ – ☐

Occasion: _________________________________

____

____

____

One Night Stand ☐   Friends With Benefits ☐

Partner ☐   Complicated ☐

How good was it - Ring in how you felt:

The best thing about this sexual encounter:_______________

____

PARTNER 97

Name:______________________________________

Age:________________

Sex:__________________

Country:______________________________

Date: ☐ ☐ ☐   Time: ☐ – ☐

Occasion:______________________________

____

____

____

One Night Stand ☐   Friends With Benefits ☐

Partner ☐   Complicated ☐

How good was it - Ring in how you felt:

The best thing about this sexual encounter: __________________

____

PARTNER 98

Name:

Age:

Sex:

Country:

WE NEED MORE INFO, HUN

Date: ☐ ☐ ☐   Time: ☐ - ☐

Occasion:

One Night Stand ☐   Friends With Benefits ☐

Partner ☐   Complicated ☐

How good was it - Ring in how you felt:

The best thing about this sexual encounter:

PARTNER 99

Name:____

Age:________________

Sex:________________

Country:_________________________________

Date: ☐ ☐ ☐   Time: ☐ – ☐

Occasion:_________________________________

____

____

____

One Night Stand ☐   Friends With Benefits ☐

Partner ☐   Complicated ☐

How good was it - Ring in how you felt:

The best thing about this sexual encounter: ________________

____

PARTNER 100

Name:____

Age:________________

Sex:__________________________

Country:____

WE NEED MORE INFO, HUN

Date: ☐ ☐ ☐   Time: ☐ – ☐

Occasion: ____

____

____

____

One Night Stand ☐   Friends With Benefits ☐

Partner ☐   Complicated ☐

How good was it - Ring in how you felt:

The best thing about this sexual encounter:________________

____

Thank you for purchasing this sex journal
and I hope you enjoyed it.

Join Lovestories Press facebook group to
stay in the know on upcoming
releases, giveaways and a better way to
connect with us!